WHY IGNORE THEM?

LET'S CONFRONT AND WIN!!

MANASI PATIL

No.8, 3rd Cross Street,CIT Colony,
Mylapore, Chennai, Tamil Nadu-600004

ISBN 978-1-64919-011-6

To Krishna, my nature-loving brother...

Contents

WHY IGNORE THEM?

LET'S CONFRONT AND WIN!!

WHY IGNORE THEM ?
LET'S CONFRONT AND WIN !!
MANASI PATIL

*"IT IS IN YOUR HAND TO CREATE A
BETTER WORLD FOR ALL WHO LIVE IN
IT"*

-Nelson Mandela

Introduction

I have often thought of writing something that inspires and helps people.

'Words are Containers of Power', I believe.

That's the reason for this book.

I've tried my hand at various writing competitions, even online, and won many of them!

Mostly, the topics included were: Fantasies, nature-based, world-based, mysteries and many more.

Then I thought, why not write a book?

I had been recently studying the topics on nature and the world and came to the conclusion that many of the important issues of the world are being ignored!!

Yes, you read it right!

There are some majorly disturbing problems, which are not the ones that come to our mind when thinking of global issues.

So, here, in 'Why Ignore Them?' I've penned down 9 of the issues shunned by the world.

Hope the writing spreads awareness in one and all, which is the need of the hour, I must say.

Since we are the cause for these issues, we must be the ones to patch it up as before...

CHAPTER ONE

RELIGIOUS CONFLICTS

Religious Conflicts is a global issue unheeded by people and a problem yet to be solved.

The spike in religious violence is global and affects every religious group.

A 2018 Minority Rights Group report indicates that mass killings and other slaughters are increasing in countries both affected and not affected by war alike.

While bloody encounters were recorded in over 50 countries, most reported lethal incidents involving minorities were concentrated in Syria, Iraq, Nigeria, India, Myanmar, Pakistan and Bangladesh.

Hostilities against Muslims and Jews also increased across Europe, as did threats against Hindus in more than 18 countries.

Making matters worse, 55 of the world's 198 countries imposed restrictions on religions, especially Egypt, Russia, India, Indonesia and Turkey.

Since the awakening of religion, wars have been fought in the name of different gods and goddesses.

Yes, religious conflicts stem from the fact that when the followers of one religion or group consider other's beliefs as inferior and false.

This promotes not only hatred but also lead to conflicts.
Get it Right:

- Accept that all the religions are different paths to the same destiny.
- Come together in peace and find our common bond, creating our new faith that we can share together, the 'Humanity Religion'.

CHAPTER TWO

CHILD AND HEALTH

Every child should be taught to expect success, someone has said.

It is well known that the learning process is involved in shaping one's personality and the way he/she deals with situations in life.

Children are key to our success, as we know. Yet many children across the world do not have even their most basic needs met.

The rate of dying children under-five remains the same, even increasing, furthermore.

Everyone will agree that poor health and nutrition among school going children has a negative impact on their education.

Child health and education go hand in hand.

Malnutrition of children leads to permanent physiological damage, known usually as "stunting".

Obviously, children who are hungry cannot concentrate and, thus, cannot learn. Children who go frequently hungry for a long time develop difficulties in their learning abilities and concentration. All because of hunger.

This means, they might not be able to achieve their academic or professional potential: a healthy child is a better learner.

Even when children are attending school, the quality of their education might be poor, or educational capacity and resources may be limited.

This means that there's a possibility they'll leave school without the necessary education.

It's estimated that approximately 600 million children are not mastering basic mathematics and literacy while at school.

Education is important for children because they are the future of the world, the pillar of the nation.

So, each and every child must be educated.

The children will stand out as future leaders to develop the nation from all the issues.

Get it right:

- Reduce the cost of education.
- Free lunch at school.
- Make studying interesting.
- Create study groups.
- Promote opening of mind.
- Donate old textbooks, stationery.

CHAPTER THREE

NATURE HARMING FESTIVALS

Hindu religion is admired and worshipped for its eco-friendliness.

There is nothing in it that harms nature.

It has developed many traditions to take care of nature, to maintain its balance, to develop gratitude towards it.

How come, then, that such a religion should become a huge threat to the environment?

Let's take the example of the Ganesha festival here.

It is almost brutality on human health and nature.

The screaming loudspeakers is an observable aspect of the pollution it creates; but it has a non-perceptible aspect also: the idols.

The God themselves are a pollution!

The leaves and flowers offered are a pollution too!

Shocking right?

Anything that gets accumulated so fast and in such a large quantity that nature's speed to degrade it cannot match with, is pollution.

This is what is happening in Ganesha festival nowadays.

The idols are usually made up of Plaster of Paris. (PoP)

As PoP is not water soluble once dried, the immersed idols do not break down.

They remain intact in rivers, wells, or seas, for months. (some good people recover them, repaint them, and sell them the next year: a good recycling!)

The colors slowly seep into water, making the water poisonous.

This is totally against the principles of Hinduism: whatever is created, must be destroyed. But the cycle of nature should never get obstructed.

That is why, the idols should be of clay. When they are immersed in water, they readily disintegrate. The material quickly becomes a part of natural cycle.

But there is one drawback.

The idol is not eco-friendly just because it is made of clay.

It may have been painted with artificial, poisonous colors. After immersion, these toxic colors get mixed in water.

This is anti-religious.

Another requirement is the size of the idols.

Big idols mean more use of clay, more transportation, more use of colors and more sedimentation. To avoid all this, 'small is beautiful'.

Due to immersion of idols and flowers by thousands of people, the water becomes dirty.

The flowers decay, leading to air and water pollution. Many wells have been totally filled with mud accumulated over the years!

The best policy, therefore, is decentralization.

Immerse the idol in a bucketful of water in your own house and after a day or two pour the mud water under any tree.

The flowers need not be immersed at all- they can be used for fertilizing.

In a nutshell, Hinduism and eco-friendliness being synonymous concepts, let us be 'religious' in the true sense of the term.

Let us be real 'fundamentalists.'

And put a stop to our deadly actions before we are forced to put a stop to our festivals.

Get it Right:

- Prepare ecofriendly colors.
- Make your own idols with clay, painted with natural dyes.
- Avoid plastics, thermocol and electric lightning.
- Avoid noise pollution

CHAPTER FOUR

COMMUNICABLE DISEASES

Communicable, or infectious diseases, are caused by microorganisms such as bacteria, viruses, parasites and fungi that can be spread, directly or indirectly, from one person to another.

Some diseases are transmitted through bites from insects, while others are caused by ingesting contaminated food or water.

Examples of the these include HIV, hepatitis A, B and C, measles, salmonella, measles, blood-borne illnesses, etc.

Increased access to clean water and awareness about proper sanitation has resulted in an overall decrease in the occurrence of transferable diseases worldwide. The importance of good nutritional education and preventing personal harm is now emphasized.

For example, explaining the dangers of a sugary diet, excessive alcohol consumption, smoking tobacco, using unsafe cooking fuels, driving recklessly, and walking across a busy highway, is essential.

In the 1970s, many experts thought that the fight against infectious diseases was over.

In fact, in 1970, the Surgeon-General of the United States of America indicated that it was "time to close the book on infectious diseases, declare the war against pestilence won, and shift national resources to such chronic problems as cancer and heart disease".

But while the focus of the global healthcare community has now shifted to non-communicable diseases, communicable diseases remain a burden in low-income countries and states.

Communicable diseases are still responsible for 71% of deaths, and low-income countries are the ones most severely affected.

Communicable diseases, alone or in combination with malnutrition, account for the greatest number of deaths in complex emergencies. They promote high incidence rates of diarrhea, respiratory infection, malaria, and measles.

Get it right:

Wash your hands often. This is especially important before and after preparing food, before eating and after using the toilet.

Get vaccinated. Immunization can reduce the chances of catching many diseases. Keep your recommended vaccinations up to date.

Stay at home if you have signs and symptoms of an infection. Don't go to work or class if you're vomiting, have diarrhea or are running a fever.

Be smart about food preparation. Keep counters and other kitchen surfaces clean when preparing meals. In addition, promptly refrigerate leftovers. Don't let cooked foods remain at room temperature for an extended period of time.

Disinfect the 'hot zones' in your residence. These include the kitchen and bathroom — two rooms that can have a high concentration of bacteria and other infectious agents.

Travel wisely. Don't fly when you're ill. With so many people confined to such a small area, you may infect other passengers in the plane. And your trip won't be comfortable, either.

Cover a cough. Cover your mouth and nose with a tissue when you sneeze or cough, then dispose of it. If no tissue is handy, cough or sneeze into your elbow rather than into your hands.

With a little common sense and the proper precautions, you can avoid infectious diseases and avoid spreading them, thus helping reduce the global threat.

13

CHAPTER FIVE

OBESITY

At the other end of the malnutrition scale, obesity is one of today's most obviously visible – yet most neglected – public health problems.

It is one of the most attention-needed global emergency.

In 2010, humanity passed an important milestone. According to the Global Burden of Disease Study, published in the journal '*The Lancet*', obesity became a bigger public-health problem than hunger.

Obesity is generally caused by eating too much and moving too little. If you consume high amounts of energy, but do not burn off the energy through exercise and physical activity, most of the additional energy will be stored by the body as fat.

Mostly, we expect obesity will only be seen among high income groups. Don't we?

But that's apparently not so.

All people are affected, no matter their income level.

Go visit your local market. Compare the price of half a kg apples and a bar of chocolate. Which would you choose if you didn't have any money?

And we all know, obesity level is increased when people consume food that is low in proteins, high in carbs and preservatives.

Certain populations tend to have higher rates of obesity.

Overweight and obesity are often accompanied by other health conditions such as diabetes, heart disease, hypertension, certain cancers, and arthritis.

Today, according to the latest edition of the study, more than 2.1 billion people—nearly 30% of the global population—are overweight or obese.

That is nearly two and a half times the number of adults and children who are undernourished. Obesity is responsible for about 5% of deaths worldwide.

This crisis is not just a persistent health concern; it is also a threat to the global economy. The total impact of obesity is about 2.8% of world GDP—roughly equal to the economic damage caused by smoking, armed violence, war, and terrorism, according to a new research by the McKinsey Global Institute (MGI).

To make matters worse, in countries with limited public-health services, the cost of health care falls right on the distressed households.

As a result, obesity can lead to poverty and spread inequality.

Preventing it plays an important role in good health. Obesity causes many chronic health conditions, many of which become difficult to treat over time.

These conditions include:

- metabolic syndrome
- type 2 diabetes
- high blood pressure

- <u>high triglycerides and low "good" cholesterol</u>
- <u>heart disease</u>
- <u>stroke</u>
- <u>sleep apnea</u>
- <u>gallbladder disease</u>
- <u>nonalcoholic fatty liver disease</u>
- <u>osteoarthritis</u>
- <u>mental health conditions</u>

For many countries, tackling obesity will require a national—if not global—effort. No single unit—government, retailers, consumer-goods companies, restaurants, employers, media organizations, educators, health-care providers, or individuals—can address obesity on its own.

An escalating global epidemic of overweight and obesity – "globesity" – is taking over many parts of the world. If immediate action is not taken, millions will suffer from an array of serious health disorders, WHO has stated.

Get it right:

Exact methods to stop the global issue have not been declared yet. But there are some ways by which we can help in reducing it.

- Avoid cars. What is better than a cycle?
- Consume 'good' fat. No 'bad' fat!

A study published in the Nutrition Journal showed that intake of healthy dietary fats, such as polyunsaturated fats, can improve cholesterol levels and reduce obesity risk.

- Eat slowly and only when hungry

The excess fuel produced eventually becomes stored as body fat and can lead to obesity.

- Go physical!

The World Health Organization (WHO) recommends that kids and teens get at least an hour of physical activity on a daily basis.

- Limit screen time.

More time spent sitting in front of a screen means less time for physical activity and good sleep. Because exercise and sleep play a role in a healthy weight, it's important to encourage outdoor activities over computer or TV time.

FOOD SECURITY

Food security is another majorly ignored world crisis.

Why is it so?

The obvious reason is that everybody needs food. But delivering enough food to a national and the whole world's population is a problem.

In short, this is a global challenge because it's not just about food and feeding people but also about practically all aspects of an economy and society.

The number of hungry people in the world has increased over the last few years. One in nine people in the world go hungry each day and suffer from deficiencies as a result.

Food security is biggest threat to overall human population, more than malaria, tuberculosis or HIV.

So, what is the problem?

How can it be 2020 and people are still going hungry?

The problem is not that we aren't producing enough food, but rather that people lack access to food.

Many people do not have enough money to purchase food and cannot grow their own.

According to the World Food Programme (WFP), <u>countries with the highest level of food insecurity</u>

<u>also have the highest outward migration of refugees</u>.

While overall hunger has steadily decreased over the past decade, there has been an increase in the number of refugees. Refugees are the ones typically suffering the most from food insecurity.

What causes it?

- Population growth- the population is growing day by day, thereby, increasing the need for food.

- Changing tastes – not only is the population growing, but its diet is changing too. As people become more well to do, they start eating food that is richer in processed foods, meat and dairy. But to produce more meat means growing more grain.

- Water scarcity – this is another important crisis: 28% of agriculture lies in water-stressed regions. It takes roughly 1,500 liters of water to produce a kilogram of wheat, and about 16,000 liters to produce a kilogram of beef. In 2050, we'll need twice as much water.

Get it right:

- Eat more plant-based foods.
- Stop food loss and waste.
- Research on avoiding food crisis and follow it.

If you
can't
feed a
hundred
people, then
just
feed
one.
one.
– mother Teresa

CHAPTER SEVEN

WATER SCARCITY

Water scarcity is the lack of available water resources to meet the demands of water usage.

It already affects every continent and around 2.8 billion people around the world suffer from water scarcity at least one month each year.

More than 1.2 billion people lack access to clean drinking water.

They are exposed to diseases, such as cholera and typhoid fever, and other water-borne illnesses.

Two million people, mostly children, die each year from diarrheal diseases alone.

As with food, there is actually enough fresh water for each person currently living on the planet.

So, what is wrong?

Access to that water is not always possible for everyone.

Issues such as poor infrastructure, displacement, and conflict mean that many people often have to use unsafe water sources.

This is a clear health and sanitation risk.

Many of the water systems that keep ecosystems thriving are facing a growing human population.

Rivers and lakes are drying up or becoming too polluted to use.

More than half the world's wetlands have disappeared.

Agriculture consumes more water than any other source and ruins much of that through wastefulness.

Climate change is changing patterns of weather and water around the world, causing shortages and droughts in some areas and floods in others.

At the current consumption rate, this situation will only get worse.

By 2025, two-thirds of the world's population may face water shortages. And ecosystems around the world will suffer even more.

Though we all rely on water for our survival, we also contribute to the rise of water scarcity. The importance of rivers, lakes, and other bodies of freshwater is endangered by a variety of causes, many of which are the result of human activity.

These include pollution, climate change, industrial agricultural practices, unmanageable energy production, and population growth. The end result is that more and more people around the globe face water scarcity.

Get it Right:

• Developing water filtration systems

It's one thing to have access to water, and it's another to have access to water that is safe to drink. Effective water filtration systems help ensure freshwater can be put to good use—not making us sick. That's one of the reasons why companies worldwide are committed to developing proper water filtration systems that produce purified water free from bacteria, microbes, and other contaminants, and bringing this clean drinking water to as many schools, hospitals, workplaces, and homes as possible.

• *Protecting wetlands*

Wetlands are natural water filtration systems. Well, that means they have a big role in collecting and purifying water. Wetlands are disappearing at an alarming rate, but conserving wetlands could have a major payoff. Currently, an international treaty called the Ramsar Convention has helped protect more than 2,000 wetlands. More aggressive conservation measures are required if we want wetlands to assist our efforts to reduce water scarcity.

- *Improving irrigation efficiency*

Industrial agriculture is one of the biggest drains on water resources. Simply switching from flood irrigation systems to sprinklers or drip irrigation systems could help the agricultural area save a tremendous amount of water. When combined with better soil management practices such as no-till or limited tillage and mulching, which reduces evaporation from the soil, more efficient irrigation systems can significantly reduce water usage.

- *Increasing water storage in reservoirs*

Climate change increases the frequency of droughts and floods. By expanding the reservoir capacity, we can capture and storage floodwater, to prevent its loss to the ocean, where it becomes salinized and more difficult to treat. This stored water can be used to provide water during times of drought.

CHAPTER EIGHT

CLIMATE CHANGE

Climate change is a change in the earth's climate. It is the difference in the earth's global climate.

Climate change is the biggest issue in today's world, yet an ignored one. People never take care until the worst starts affecting them.

Climate change can be warmer or colder. This includes global warming and global cooling. Climate change has also related to other damaging weather events such as more frequent and intense hurricanes, floods, downpours and winter storms we are facing today.

The causes of current climate change are burning of natural gas which produces, what we call, greenhouses gases. Climate change is caused by water vapor, carbon dioxide, the deathly methane, nitrous oxide, chlorofluorocarbons, etc. released and caused by humans.

Climate change affects us in many ways. Not only us, but everything that is present on this living world, the Earth.

The direct consequences we can observe are as follows:

- Rising hot and cold temperature.

- Increasing sea levels.
- Higher ocean temperatures.
- An increase in heavy rainfall, hailstorms, etc.
- Melting and shrinking glaciers.

Also, there is a bigger reason for this climate change:

The more a person uses or wastes resources, the bigger he is.

The more he pollutes, thee higher is his status.

How? you ask?

A cyclist doesn't use any fuel, neither does he pollute. So, he is a common man.

As soon as he purchases a motor bike, his lifestyle changes. When he buys a car---thereby consuming more fuel and polluting more--- his greatness upsurges further.

One who bathes in half a bucket water, is a small man. But he who sits under a shower for hours is a big shot!

He who switches off unwanted lamps or fans, is a miser: he who keeps such equipment unnecessarily 'on' is looked towards with admiration.

If he goes for coolers and ACs, instead of fans, his status further uplifts.

The moral: More the ecologically harmful one's living, more the contribution towards climate change, the greater is a person's image in the society. Those who are wealthy are thus constantly 'desiring'

But although one has money to spend unsparingly, does nature have so many resources or energies? Does it have the capacity to absorb so much of pollution and waste? Does it have unlimited resources? No, it doesn't, my friends.

Remembering this, we must put a stop to our flexibility. We should not be a burden to the environment. If we do a bit of analysis and be a little far-sighted, we can reduce this burden greatly and at one stage, get rid of it entirely. Or else there will be no saying what can happen to the future generation. People are ignoring this fact frankly and are using the nature as they wish.

In the lockdown of 2020, due to the COVID-19, we can observe a great change on the earth. The climate has drastically taken a turn. In a good way that is.

But what are our measures to keep it the same way after the release of the lockdown?

'I can afford; hence I'll uses as much water/electricity/natural gases as I wish' is just an arrogance.

You can afford--- nature can't.

Get it Right:

- Be a Vegetarian:

It is estimated that meat is responsible for 15-18% of climate changing emission. Too much meat can also be bad for a person's health, study shows. It also puts a stress on already over-exerted health services due to the lockdown. So, where possible, have some meat-free days. Become more self-sufficient by eating veg.

- Never cease to recycle

Fashion industry is responsible for more carbon emissions than the air and marine industries combined. Did you know that? So, instead of buying new, make the most of what you have, upcycle you wardrobe, friends!!

- Reduce food waste:

Food security is another major problem in this world. While you are wasting food in your house, there are people struggling for it and some even dying due to the lack of it. So, don't waste your food. Use leftovers when you can. If you have cooked something extra, donate it to a needy one, instead of donating it to the garbage.

- Reduce emissions

Bought a car? Your image must have increased so much in the society then, hasn't it? But in the eyes of the nature, your value has decreased, my friend. Vehicles release many harmful gases that are toxic to the nature as well as your near and dear ones. And no, I'm not saying 'no' to the use of cars, motorbikes.

But whenever possible, just avoid it. Why use a car when going to visit the market, if it is near you? Use a bicycle. To

emissions and pollutions, bicycle is the only solution.

* Save Energy

I know Summer can be unbearably hot. But you are making the future even more scorching by using the AC. The air conditioners we use releases CFC's which are as deadly as they can be. Why burn the future?
Avoid AC's- that's the message.

* The 3R's

Reduce, Reuse and Recycle...
What's better than that? We all know them but it's just that we fail to implement them in our day-to-day life. Let us all be the 3R users!

* Plant a tree!

Planting a tree not only helps you by giving an unlimited supply of oxygen, but also saves your future.
Each one, Plant one.
And then, see the result! Greenery everywhere! Oxygen! Flowers! Fruits!
That's the best deal and offer ever made or ever going to be!

ONLINE EDUCATION

The nationwide lockdown required to contain the spread of COVID-19 has pushed hundreds of schools to move their classes online.

Suddenly, lakhs of children are spending a large portion of their time online.

One of the most evident issues with online education is the lack of social communication. If an online course has any sort of discussion, it is usually a written discussion in the form of an online post.

For students looking to become successful outside the classroom in any career that requires verbal communication skills, this could be considered a substantial drawback.

Many at-risk students are behind in reading and math. If they are using online courses to "catch up," they may find themselves faltering for further explanation or involvement when they don't grasp a concept.

Some online courses consist of pre-programmed software that has the student read or listen to a lecture and then take a test or quiz.

The computer (or software) scores the tests and either passes the student on or not.

If these courses are not closely managed, what keeps students from cheating or having someone who can read and understand the content better take the tests for them?

Drawbacks of online education:

Can't ask questions: In an online class, students cannot raise their hands and ask a question when they are confused by the material.

Can't pace the lecture: In a regular lecture, the teacher can tell when students are not following the subject and adjust the pace accordingly. But in an online course that is not possible.

Loss of the group experience: There's something about watching a movie with a large group of people that is different from watching it all alone. Same for the classroom, it's a group experience. When a lecture is live in a classroom rather than at home on video there are no interruptions from parents, siblings, there is no refrigerator calling your name, you don't have the choice to delay and put it the work until later, etc.

A classroom commands your attention in a way that videos do not.

While some have expressed alarm about the potential dangers of internet exposure for young children, others say they are scared the digital shift may separate economically disadvantaged students who don't have access to the technology online education require.

On 15 April 2020, the United Nations Children's Fund (UNICEF), which is engaged in charitable aid for children around the globe, said, 'millions of children are at an increased risk of harm as their lives move increasingly online during lockdown in the Covid-19 pandemic".

Acknowledgements

As Alfred North Whitehead has rightly said,
"No one who achieves success does so without
acknowledging the help of others. The wise and confident
acknowledge this help with gratitude."
I too, greatly acknowledge and appreciate the help of
all those who helped me create my first book.
I sincerely thank the following people—
My Parents, Mahesh and Gauri - For teaching me all
that I know. I owe everything to them. Thank you Aai and
Baba...
My Little Brother, Krishna- Just for being Krishna.
Thank you for always caring for me and helping me. Your
smile is my energy!!
My Grandmother, Nirmala- For piquing an interest in
me for stories and tales. And for being my childhood
storyteller...Thank you Aaji...
And how can I ever forget you, dear reader, for picking
up 'WHY IGNORE THEM?'?
Thank you everyone from the depth of my heart!!!

About The Author

The best place to start is the beginning, it's said.
Manasi has started her author journey right from the age of 5, an age when others are busy playing!
She is very passionate about reading and writing and has her own 'mini library' at her house.
She has also written many unpublished stories and poems.
Manasi is also the author of 'The Cousins Crime' a fun and thrilling mystery to read...
She also enjoys playing guitar and is a great lover of nature. The 14year old tries her best to resolve the issues nature is facing.
And if it is possible, Manasi will spend an entire day in the nature, greenery, curled up reading her favorite book.

Thank you for reading my book!
Love it?
Then don't forget to leave a review on amazon or
wherever you purchased the book!
Every review matters to me, and it matters a lot!

*I really appreciate all your feedback and I love hearing
what you have to say.
I need your input to make my future books even better!
Thanks so much!*
-Manasi Patil

Read More...

Available on Amazon.com and other Amazon
marketplaces! In kindle format + paperback !
A thrilling, mind-blowing mystery!

THE COUSINS CRIME